MY FIRST KNOCK KNOCK JOKE BOOK

www.randomhousechildrens.co.uk

Other Young Corgi Books to get your teeth into:

My First Knock Knock Joke Book

Scoular Anderson

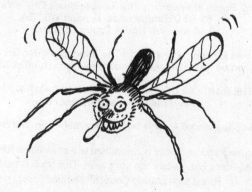

YOUNG CORGI

MY FIRST KNOCK KNOCK JOKE BOOK
A YOUNG CORGI BOOK 9780552546928

PRINTING HISTORY
Young Corgi edition published 2001

25

Set in 15/19pt Univers

Young Corgi Books are published by Random House Children's Publishers UK, 61–63 Uxbridge Road, London W5 5SA, A Random House Group Company

Addresses for companies within The Random House Group Limited can be found at: www.randomhouse.co.uk/offices.htm

THE RANDOM HOUSE GROUP Limited Reg. No. 954009
www.**randomhousechildrens**.co.uk

A CIP catalogue record for this book is available from the British Library.

Penguin Random House is committed to a sustainable future for our business, our readers and our planet. This book is made from Forest Stewardship Council® certified paper.

Printed and bound in Great Britain by Clays Ltd, Elcograf S.p.A.

For Fin and Maddie

Knock knock!
Who's there?
Ketchup.
Ketchup who?
Ketchup with me and I'll tell you!

Knock knock!
Who's there?
Lee King.
Lee King who?
Lee King bucket.

Knock knock!
Who's there?
Boo.
Boo who?
Don't cry, it's only a joke!

Knock knock!
Who's there?
Roland.
Roland who?
Roland butter, please.

Knock knock!
Who's there?
Lois.
Lois who?
Lois the opposite of high.

Knock knock!
Who's there?
Howard.
Howard who?
Howard you like a ride in my car?

Knock knock!
Who's there?
Patsy.
Patsy who?
Patsy nice dog on the head.

13

Knock knock!
Who's there?
Ice cream.
Ice cream who?
Ice cream and scream until you
open the door.

Knock knock!
Who's there?
Bernadette.
Bernadette who?
Bernadette all my dinner!

Knock knock!
Who's there?
Stan.
Stan who?
Stan back! I'm breaking the door down!

Knock knock!
Who's there?
Dozen.
Dozen who?
Dozen anybody want to play with me?

Knock knock!
Who's there?
Rosa.
Rosa who?
Rosa carrots growing in your garden.

Knock knock!
Who's there?
Sultan.
Sultan who?
Sultan pepper.

Knock knock!
Who's there?
Mister.
Mister who?
Mister last bus home.

Knock knock!
Who's there?
Waddle.
Waddle who?
Waddle you give me for these
old toys?

Knock knock!
Who's there?
Watson.
Watson who?
Watson your head?

Knock knock!
Who's there?
Who.
Who who?
I'm sorry, I don't talk to owls.

Knock knock!
Who's there?
Thistle.
Thistle who?
Thistle be the last time I bring you
flowers.

Knock knock!
Who's there?
Lettuce.
Lettuce who?
Lettuce in – it's wet out here!

Knock knock!
Who's there?
Punch.
Punch who?
Not me, please!

Knock knock!
Who's there?
Romeo.
Romeo who?
Romeo-ver to the other side
of the lake.

Knock knock!
Who's there?
Tuna.
Tuna who?
Tuna violin and it will sound better.

Knock knock!
Who's there?
Pudding.
Pudding who?
Pudding on your shoes before your
trousers is a bad idea.

Knock knock!
Who's there?
Martin.
Martin who?
Martin of biscuits is empty.

Knock knock!
Who's there?
Andrew.
Andrew who?
Andrew all over the wall so now
there'll be trouble!

Knock knock!
Who's there?
Ewan.
Ewan who?
Nobody else, just me.

Knock knock!
Who's there?
Island.
Island who?
Island on your roof with my
parachute.

Knock knock!
Who's there?
Isadore.
Isadore who?
Isadore not better than a gate?

Knock knock!
Who's there?
Tuba.
Tuba who?
Tuba toothpaste on the doorstep.

Knock knock!
Who's there?
Justin.
Justin who?
Justin case the dog howls,
leave him outside.

Knock knock!
Who's there?
Lucy.
Lucy who?
Lucy-lastic can be very embarrassing.

Knock knock!
Who's there?
Buster.
Buster who?
Buster the town centre leaves every hour.

Knock knock!
Who's there?
Yah.
Yah who?
Yahoo! Ride 'em cowboy!

Knock knock!
Who's there?
Amos.
Amos who?
Amos-quito just bit me!

Knock knock!
Who's there?
Howell.
Howell who?
Howell you have your toast – with marmalade or jam?

Knock knock!
Who's there?
Felix.
Felix who?
Felix my lolly again, I'll thump him!

Knock knock!
Who's there?
Omar.
Omar who?
Omar goodness! Wrong door!

Knock knock!
Who's there?
Ella.
Ella who?
Ella-phants are dancing on your lawn.

Knock knock!
Who's there?
Luke.
Luke who?
Luke through the keyhole
and you'll see!

Knock knock!
Who's there?
Roxanne.
Roxanne who?
Roxanne pebbles all over the beach.

Knock knock!
Who's there?
Lionel.
Lionel who?
Lionel roar when he's hungry.

Knock knock!
Who's there?
Athena.
Athena who?
Athena hippo in your garden.

Knock knock!
Who's there?
Doughnut.
Doughnut who?
Doughnut open your presents until
Christmas Day!

Knock knock!
Who's there?
Al.
Al who?
Al go home if you don't open
the door now.

Knock knock!
Who's there?
Doris.
Doris who?
Doris dropping off its hinges with all
this knocking!

Knock knock!
Who's there?
Lydia.
Lydia who?
Lydia dustbin just flew away.

Knock knock!
Who's there?
Rabbit.
Rabbit who?
Rabbit up nicely, it's a present.

Knock knock!
Who's there?
Ivor.
Ivor who?
Ivor good mind to get you a doorbell,
so I don't have to do all this knocking!

Knock knock!
Who's there?
Eggs.
Eggs who?
Eggs-tremely cold, hurry up and open
the door!

Knock knock!
Who's there?
Walter.
Walter who?
Walter wall carpeting.

Knock knock!
Who's there?
Egbert.
Egbert who?
Egbert no bacon.

Knock knock!
Who's there?
Cows go.
Cows go who?
No, silly, cows go moo!

Knock knock!
Who's there?
Danielle.
Danielle who?
Danielle so loud, we can hear you
from here!

Knock knock!
Who's there?
Juno.
Juno who?
Juno what time it is?

Knock knock!
Who's there?
Irish stew.
Irish stew who?
Irish stew in the name of the law.

Knock knock!
Who's there?
Olive.
Olive who?
Olive just round the corner.

Knock knock!
Who's there?
Russian.
Russian who?
Russian around has tired me out.

Knock knock!
Who's there?
Sofa.
Sofa who?
Sofa, we haven't managed to reach
the bell.

Knock knock!
Who's there?
Eve.
Eve who?
Eve ho my hearties!

Knock knock!
Who's there?
Arthur.
Arthur who?
Arthur Mometer is good for
measuring temperature.

Knock knock!
Who's there?
Kanga.
Kanga who?
No, it's kangaROO!

Knock knock!
Who's there?
Isabel.
Isabel who?
Isabel necessary on a bicycle?

Knock knock!
Who's there?
Handsome.
Handsome who?
Handsome sweets through the letter box!

Knock knock!
Who's there?
Barbara.
Barbara who?
Barbara black sheep, have you
any wool?

Knock knock!
Who's there?
Tish.
Tish who?
Bless you!

MY FIRST JOKE BOOK
Scoular Anderson

What is the crocodile's favourite game?
Snap!

How do you start a teddy-bear race?
Ready, teddy, go!

Full of brilliant jokes and
funny pictures just for you – get
My First Joke Book now and start
giggling!

ISBN 0 552 542784

YOUNG CORGI

SAMMY'S SUPER SEASON
Lindsay Camp

A cat who can play football?!

Harry's cat, Sammy, is no ordinary tabby – he's the star goalkeeper of the school football team. And it's not just Harry and his school-mates who are fans. Sammy's spectacular saves attract the attention of Mudchester United FC. Will Sammy be tempted to play in the Premiership, or would he rather be at home eating Katbix?

A very funny story about an amazing footballing cat – perfect for building reading confidence.

ISBN 0 552 546615

DOG MAGIC!
Chris Priestley

Imagine being able to wish for anything you wanted!

Lucy has the surprise of her life when she releases a genie from an old bottle. Wow – unlimited wishes for a year! But wait a minute. . . Lucy didn't wish for dinosaur bones. And where have all the cats gone?

Why does Lucy's dog Mitch look so full of himself? *Uh-oh*. It looks like a case of dog magic!

Young Corgi books are perfect for building reading confidence.

ISBN 0 552 546887

YOUNG CORGI